The
Bible Promise
Book® *for*
BAD DAYS

The
Bible Promise
Book® *for*
BAD DAYS

Inspiration and Encouragement for Kids

BY JEAN FISCHER

BARBOUR BOOKS
An Imprint of Barbour Publishing, Inc.

© 2019 by Barbour Publishing, Inc.

ISBN 978-1-68322-843-1

All rights reserved. No part of this publication may be reproduced or transmitted for commercial purposes, except for brief quotations in printed reviews, without written permission of the publisher.

Churches and other noncommercial interests may reproduce portions of this book without the express written permission of Barbour Publishing, provided that the text does not exceed 500 words or 5 percent of the entire book, whichever is less, and that the text is not material quoted from another publisher. When reproducing text from this book, include the following credit line: "From *The Bible Promise Book® for Bad Days: Inspiration and Encouragement for Kids*, published by Barbour Publishing, Inc. Used by permission."

Scripture quotations are taken from the New Life Version (NLV) copyright © 1969 and 2003 by Barbour Publishing, Inc. All rights reserved.

Published by Barbour Books, an imprint of Barbour Publishing Inc., 1810 Barbour Drive, Uhrichsville, Ohio 44683, www.barbourbooks.com

Our mission is to inspire the world with the life-changing message of the Bible.

Printed in the United States of America.

06353   0119   SP

CONTENTS

INTRODUCTION

God, please help!
I've had a terrible, horrible,
no good, very bad day!

When it feels as though you've had the WORST. DAY. EVER. and *nothing* has gone right. . .

Maybe you spoke some words you wish you could take back.

Maybe you got picked on by the school bully.

Or maybe you just woke up feeling like a grumpy old grouch today.

Whatever it is that turned your day from right-side-up to upside down, God knows and He cares. And He has a lot to say about it in His Word, the Bible.

Did you know that the Bible is full of God's promises just for you? And if you take time to read and think about those promises, a "worst day ever" can have a wonderful turnaround. It's true!

The Bible Promise Book® *for Bad Days* is overflowing with words of love from the heavenly Father and just the wisdom you need to get through those hard days—with hope in your heart and a smile on your face.

Read on to turn your day right-side-up again!

I'M MAD AT MOM OR DAD.

So, you're mad at Mom or Dad. Even worse—maybe you're mad at BOTH of your parents.

It's hard to know what to do, right? Especially when you'd like nothing more than to throw an epic temper tantrum that they won't soon forget. After all, you're super-duper angry!

What can you do to get those out-of-control angry feelings to go away?

When it feels like it's impossible to be nice and obedient, and you're not so sure you can get over your fuming feelings, here's what God's Word has to say about that. . .

"Honor your father and your mother, so your life may be long in the land the Lord your God gives you."

Exodus 20:12

Children, as Christians, obey your parents. This is the right thing to do.

Ephesians 6:1

Hear your father's teaching, my son, and do not turn away from your mother's teaching. For they are a glory to your head and a chain of beauty around your neck.

Proverbs 1:8–9

Put out of your life all these things: bad feelings about other people, anger, temper, loud talk, bad talk which hurts other people, and bad feelings which hurt other people.

Ephesians 4:31

The Lord will give His people peace.

Psalm 29:11

He who is slow to anger is better than the powerful. And he who rules his spirit is better than he who takes a city.

PROVERBS 16:32

He who is slow to get angry has great understanding, but he who has a quick temper makes his foolish way look right.

PROVERBS 14:29

Do all things without arguing and talking about how you wish you did not have to do them.

PHILIPPIANS 2:14

Most of all, have a true love for each other. Love covers many sins.

1 PETER 4:8

Live in peace with each other. Do not act or think with pride. . . . Keep yourself from thinking you are so wise.

ROMANS 12:16

Every one of you must have respect for his mother and his father. . . . I am the Lord your God.

LEVITICUS 19:3

A gentle answer turns away anger, but a sharp word causes anger.

PROVERBS 15:1

You must be kind to each other. Think of the other person. Forgive other people just as God forgave you because of Christ's death on the cross.

EPHESIANS 4:32

Let your father and mother be glad, and let her who gave birth to you be full of joy.

PROVERBS 23:25

A heart that has peace is life to the body, but wrong desires are like the wasting away of the bones.

PROVERBS 14:30

If the Holy Spirit is the boss over your mind, it leads to life and peace.

Romans 8:6

A man's understanding makes him slow to anger. It is to his honor to forgive and forget a wrong done to him.

Proverbs 19:11

For You are good and ready to forgive, O Lord. You are rich in loving-kindness to all who call to You.

Psalm 86:5

Put out of your life these things also: anger, bad temper, bad feelings toward others, talk that hurts people. . .

Colossians 3:8

A man who hurts people tempts his neighbor to do the same, and leads him in a way that is not good.

Proverbs 16:29

Do not be quick in spirit to be angry. For anger is in the heart of fools.

ECCLESIASTES 7:9

Wise men turn away anger.

PROVERBS 29:8

The Lord is full of loving-favor and pity, slow to anger and great in loving-kindness.

PSALM 145:8

If you are angry, do not let it become sin. Get over your anger before the day is finished.

EPHESIANS 4:26

Stop being angry. Turn away from fighting. Do not trouble yourself. It leads only to wrong-doing.

PSALM 37:8

Hate starts fights, but love covers all sins.

PROVERBS 10:12

A dry piece of food with peace and quiet is better than a house full of food with fighting.

PROVERBS 17:1

God is helping you obey Him. God is doing what He wants done in you.

PHILIPPIANS 2:13

Children, obey your parents in everything. The Lord is pleased when you do.

COLOSSIANS 3:20

So give yourselves to God. Stand against the devil and he will run away from you.

JAMES 4:7

God, please help! I've had a terrible, horrible, no good, very bad day! I am super angry at Mom and Dad.

I know they love me and want what's best for me. But it's just so hard to see things their way. Please help to calm my temper so I can react in a way that's pleasing to You, God. I want to honor You through my actions. And I really do want to honor my parents too. Fill my thoughts with wisdom from Your Word. And fill my heart with Your peace. I promise to try harder and to work on my sometimes-out-of-control emotions. I know I can do better with Your help. Thank You, God! Amen.

I GOT A BAD GRADE AT SCHOOL.

It happened. You got a bad grade at school. You did your best. . .or maybe you could have tried a little harder. Whatever! Either way, you wish that bad grade could just disappear, because it turned your perfectly good day upside down.

You might not feel so great about yourself right now—maybe you're even comparing yourself to someone who got a good grade and wishing you would have done better. (Which only makes you feel worse!)

When you get down on yourself and feel like giving up, remember this: God loves you *no matter what*! Just hang in there, and plan to do better tomorrow.

Let's take a look at what God's Word has to say. . .

For I know that nothing can keep us from the love of God. Death cannot! Life cannot! Angels cannot! Leaders cannot! Any other power cannot! Hard things now or in the future cannot!

Romans 8:38

"But you be strong. Do not lose strength of heart. For you will be paid for your work."

2 Chronicles 15:7

Keep yourselves in the love of God.

Jude 1:21

Give thanks to the God of heaven, for His loving-kindness lasts forever.

Psalm 136:26

The Lord will finish the work He started for me. O Lord, Your loving-kindness lasts forever. Do not turn away from the works of Your hands.

Psalm 138:8

But we have power over all these things through Jesus Who loves us so much.

ROMANS 8:37

The loving-kindness of God lasts all day long.

PSALM 52:1

I can do all things because Christ gives me the strength.

PHILIPPIANS 4:13

"Do not fear, for I am with you. Do not be afraid, for I am your God. I will give you strength, and for sure I will help you. Yes, I will hold you up with My right hand that is right and good."

ISAIAH 41:10

Even before the world was made, God chose us for Himself because of His love. He planned that we should be holy and without blame as He sees us.

EPHESIANS 1:4

Jesus looked at them and said, "This cannot be done by men but God can do anything."

MARK 10:27

When he falls, he will not be thrown down, because the Lord holds his hand.

PSALM 37:24

We are pressed on every side, but we still have room to move. We are often in much trouble, but we never give up.

2 CORINTHIANS 4:8

Do not let yourselves get tired of doing good. If we do not give up, we will get what is coming to us at the right time.

GALATIANS 6:9

We have come to know and believe the love God has for us. God is love. If you live in love, you live by the help of God and God lives in you.

1 JOHN 4:16

For wisdom will come into your heart. And much learning will be pleasing to your soul.

Proverbs 2:10

Be happy in your hope. Do not give up when trouble comes. Do not let anything stop you from praying.

Romans 12:12

I pray that you will know the love of Christ. His love goes beyond anything we can understand. I pray that you will be filled with God Himself.

Ephesians 3:19

The man who does not give up when tests come is happy.

James 1:12

We know that God makes all things work together for the good of those who love Him and are chosen to be a part of His plan.

Romans 8:28

God has chosen you. You are holy and loved by Him.

COLOSSIANS 3:12

People make it hard for us, but we are not left alone. We are knocked down, but we are not destroyed.

2 CORINTHIANS 4:9

You should be happy when you have all kinds of tests. You know these prove your faith. It helps you not to give up.

JAMES 1:2–3

When we have learned not to give up, it shows we have stood the test. When we have stood the test, it gives us hope.

ROMANS 5:4

An understanding mind gets much learning, and the ear of the wise listens for much learning.

PROVERBS 18:15

For the God Who is right and good tests both the hearts and the minds.

Psalm 7:9

The Lord your God is with you, a Powerful One Who wins the battle. He will have much joy over you. With His love He will give you new life. He will have joy over you with loud singing.

Zephaniah 3:17

God, I came home from school feeling unhappy. I got a bad grade, and I can't stop thinking about it. I don't feel so good about myself right now.

I know You love me no matter what. But truthfully, sometimes I don't love myself. That one bad grade made me think I should have done better. Sometimes I'm even jealous of my friends who get better grades than I do.

God, please help me to remember that all You ask of me is to do my best. And if my best isn't perfect, that's okay! Fill my heart up with Your love, and show me how to love myself more. After all, You made me—and in Your sight, I'm awesome! Amen.

THINGS JUST AREN'T GOING MY WAY.

It's one of those days. . .the kind when everything you do seems to backfire. From the moment you crawled out of bed this morning, things started going wrong. Little stuff—like misplacing your backpack, not getting your hair to look right, almost being late for school . . . Big stuff—like having an argument with your best friend, forgetting to do your homework, your team losing an important game. . .

You might even wish you could crawl back into bed, hide under the covers, and start all over—TOMORROW!

When things just aren't going your way, check out God's Word. There's plenty of wisdom in its pages to help you feel better—and even turn a bad day to good. Turn the page, and see for yourself!

This is the day that the Lord has made. Let us be full of joy and be glad in it.

PSALM 118:24

"Do not be afraid! Be strong, and see how the Lord will save you today."

EXODUS 14:13

"But you who stayed faithful to the Lord your God are all alive today."

DEUTERONOMY 4:4

"It may be that the Lord will look upon my trouble and return good to me."

2 SAMUEL 16:12

Be strong with the Lord's strength.

EPHESIANS 6:10

O Lord, You will keep us. You will keep us safe forever from the people of this day.

PSALM 12:7

"So let your whole heart be true to the Lord our God. Walk in His Laws and keep His Word, just as you are doing today."

1 Kings 8:61

For God is with the people of this day who do what is right and good.

Psalm 14:5

"So know this day, take it to your heart, that the Lord is God in the heavens above and on the earth below. There is no other."

Deuteronomy 4:39

But they who wait upon the Lord will get new strength. They will rise up with wings like eagles. They will run and not get tired. They will walk and not become weak.

Isaiah 40:31

In everything give thanks. This is what God wants you to do because of Christ Jesus.

1 Thessalonians 5:18

"Call on Me in the day of trouble. I will take you out of trouble, and you will honor Me."

PSALM 50:15

Jesus Christ is the same yesterday and today and forever.

HEBREWS 13:8

God is faithful. He will not allow you to be tempted more than you can take. But when you are tempted, He will make a way for you to keep from falling into sin.

1 CORINTHIANS 10:13

For in the day of trouble He will keep me safe in His holy tent. In the secret place of His tent He will hide me. He will set me high upon a rock.

PSALM 27:5

We are glad for our troubles also. We know that troubles help us learn not to give up.

ROMANS 5:3

"I have told you these things so you may have peace in Me. In the world you will have much trouble. But take hope! I have power over the world!"

JOHN 16:33

I will call to You in the day of my trouble. For You will answer me.

PSALM 86:7

"They came upon me in the day of my trouble. But the Lord held me up."

2 SAMUEL 22:19

"The Lord is the One Who goes before you. He will be with you. He will be faithful to you and will not leave you alone. Do not be afraid or troubled."

DEUTERONOMY 31:8

You will not be afraid of trouble at night, or of the arrow that flies by day.

PSALM 91:5

In the day of well-being be happy. But in the day of trouble, think about this: God has made the one as well as the other, so that man can never know what is going to happen.

ECCLESIASTES 7:14

May the Lord answer you in the day of trouble! May the name of the God of Jacob keep you safe.

PSALM 20:1

God is our safe place and our strength. He is always our help when we are in trouble.

PSALM 46:1

Jesus answered him, "You do not understand now what I am doing but you will later."

JOHN 13:7

He gives strength to the weak. And He gives power to him who has little strength.

ISAIAH 40:29

"The Lord will fight for you. All you have to do is keep still."

Exodus 14:14

The Lord also keeps safe those who suffer. He is a safe place in times of trouble.

Psalm 9:9

"For this day is holy to our Lord. Do not be sad for the joy of the Lord is your strength."

Nehemiah 8:10

A glad heart is good medicine, but a broken spirit dries up the bones.

Proverbs 17:22

I need You, God! Everything is upside down today. What's supposed to be good turns out bad, and I don't know what to do about it! Whatever I do, it's like the whole world is against me!

I want to stop worrying about what bad thing might happen next. I know You are with me. It helps that You know everything that's going on in my life, and You will keep me safe.

Will You please help me to see the good in things today? I want my heart to be happy. This bad day won't last forever—it's only for a little while. So, God, will You get me through it? I promise to do my very best to think about You today—and not let all the bad stuff get to me. I trust You. Amen.

MY FRIEND AND I AREN'T GETTING ALONG.

You were best friends, and now you wonder if you're friends at all. What's up with that?

It's awkward, right? When you and your best friend are hardly even speaking—or maybe you're not speaking at all. A part of you wants to stay angry; and a part of you wants to make up. The feelings inside you are churning. . .like in a blender. They're spinning wildly. You're fuming, sorry, sad, nervous. . . maybe even a little confused—ALL AT ONCE!

What can you do to make things better?

When you've had an epic falling out with a friend and when you don't know how—or even whether—to make up, God's Word can help.

A man who has friends must be a friend, but there is a friend who stays nearer than a brother.

PROVERBS 18:24

They will not stay true to their friends. They will act without thinking. They will think too much of themselves. They will love fun instead of loving God. They will do things to make it look as if they are Christians. But they will not receive the power that is for a Christian. Keep away from such people.

2 TIMOTHY 3:4–5

Dear friends, if God loved us that much, then we should love each other.

1 JOHN 4:11

Now when Job's three friends heard of all this trouble that had come upon him, they came each from his own place. . . . They agreed to meet together to come to share Job's sorrow and comfort him.

JOB 2:11

A friend loves at all times. A brother is born to share troubles.

PROVERBS 17:17

Dear friends, let us love each other, because love comes from God. Those who love are God's children and they know God.

1 JOHN 4:7

Shaking milk makes butter, and hitting the nose brings blood. So fighting comes because of anger.

PROVERBS 30:33

Dear friends, if our heart does not say that we are wrong, we will have no fear as we stand before Him.

1 JOHN 3:21

Let me say it again. Have nothing to do with foolish talk and those who want to argue. It can only lead to trouble.

2 TIMOTHY 2:23

The Lord returned to Job all the things that he had lost, when he prayed for his friends.

JOB 42:10

He will save my soul in peace from those who make war against me.

PSALM 55:18

No one can have greater love than to give his life for his friends.

JOHN 15:13

He does not hurt others with his tongue, or do wrong to his neighbor, or bring shame to his friend.

PSALM 15:3

Turn away from the sinful things young people want to do. Go after what is right. Have a desire for faith and love and peace. Do this with those who pray to God from a clean heart.

2 TIMOTHY 2:22

Iron is made sharp with iron, and one man is made sharp by a friend.

PROVERBS 27:17

Pray and give thanks for those who make trouble for you. Yes, pray for them instead of talking against them.

ROMANS 12:14

Oil and perfume make the heart glad, so are a man's words sweet to his friend.

PROVERBS 27:9

"I give you a new Law. You are to love each other. You must love each other as I have loved you. If you love each other, all men will know you are My followers."

JOHN 13:34–35

Christian brothers, never pay back someone for the bad he has done to you. Let the anger of God take care of the other person.

ROMANS 12:19

He who tells of trouble separates good friends.

PROVERBS 17:9

I am a friend to all who fear You and of those who keep Your Law.

PSALM 119:63

Love each other as Christian brothers. Show respect for each other.

ROMANS 12:10

If you think of me as a true friend, take him back as you would take me.

PHILEMON 1:17

A man with a bad temper starts fights, but he who is slow to anger quiets fighting.

PROVERBS 15:18

It is an honor for a man to keep away from fighting, but any fool will argue.

PROVERBS 20:3

A man of anger starts fights, and a man with a bad temper is full of wrong-doing.

PROVERBS 29:22

Those who make peace are happy, because they will be called the sons of God.

MATTHEW 5:9

One who hurts people with bad talk separates good friends.

PROVERBS 16:28

What starts wars and fights among you? Is it not because you want many things and are fighting to have them?

JAMES 4:1

Work for the things that make peace and help each other become stronger Christians.

ROMANS 14:19

Dear God, I don't know what to do. My friend and I had a fight, and now we're not speaking. It's weird and awkward, and I hate feeling this way.

I'm not sure which of us is right or wrong, or even if that matters right now. I need You to guide me, so I can undo some of this mess. I love my friend, and I want us both to be happy, but it's hard to be a peacemaker when I'm still angry. So help me to let go of my anger. Then please provide me with courage to have a conversation with my friend so we can make up. Give me the right words to say to turn things around. Thank You, God. Amen.

I MADE A BAD DECISION.

You messed up. You had a decision to make, and you chose wrong. . . .

Now what?! You can't undo what's been done, but you *can* trust God to take a bad decision and turn it into something good. In fact, His Word says: "We know that God makes all things work together for the good of those who love Him and are chosen to be a part of His plan" (Romans 8:28). And a lot of "the good" has to do with gaining wisdom (so you don't make the same wrong choice again), forgiving yourself, and having the right attitude.

Know this: making a bad decision doesn't mean you're a bad kid! Remember, everybody messes up sometimes. Here's what God's Word has to say about decisions. . .

If you do not have wisdom, ask God for it. He is always ready to give it to you and will never say you are wrong for asking.

JAMES 1:5

Happy is the man who finds wisdom, and the man who gets understanding. For it is better than getting silver and fine gold.

PROVERBS 3:13–14

Be careful that no one changes your mind and faith by much learning and big sounding ideas. Those things are what men dream up. They are always trying to make new religions. These leave out Christ.

COLOSSIANS 2:8

The way of a fool is right in his own eyes, but a wise man listens to good teaching.

PROVERBS 12:15

I hurried and did not wait to obey Your Law.

PSALM 119:60

The beginning of wisdom is: Get wisdom!
And with all you have gotten, get
understanding.

Proverbs 4:7

A wise son listens when his father tells him
the right way, but one who laughs at the
truth does not listen when strong words are
spoken to him.

Proverbs 13:1

The earth is full of Your loving-kindness,
O Lord. Teach me Your Law.

Psalm 119:64

If we say that we have no sin, we lie to ourselves and the truth is not in us.

1 John 1:8

Listen to words about what you should do,
and take your punishment if you need it, so
that you may be wise the rest of your days.

Proverbs 19:20

Teach me what I should know to be right and fair for I believe in Your Law.

Psalm 119:66

"Lord is slow to anger and filled with loving-kindness, forgiving sin and wrong-doing."

Numbers 14:18

Tell your sins to each other. And pray for each other so you may be healed. The prayer from the heart of a man right with God has much power.

James 5:16

But you must be sorry for your sins and turn from them. You must turn to God and have your sins taken away. Then many times your soul will receive new strength from the Lord.

Acts 3:19

Who can see his own mistakes? Forgive my sins that I do not see.

Psalm 19:12

Let the sinful turn from his way, and the one who does not know God turn from his thoughts. Let him turn to the Lord, and He will have loving-pity on him. Let him turn to our God, for He will for sure forgive all his sins.

Isaiah 55:7

For a man who is right with God falls seven times, and rises again, but the sinful fall in time of trouble.

Proverbs 24:16

We all make many mistakes.

James 3:2

So now tell your sins to the Lord God of your fathers, and do His will.

Ezra 10:11

So be careful how you live. Live as men who are wise and not foolish.

Ephesians 5:15

Trust in the Lord with all your heart, and do not trust in your own understanding. Agree with Him in all your ways, and He will make your paths straight.

Proverbs 3:5–6

You are a forgiving God. You are kind and loving, slow to anger, and full of loving-kindness.

Nehemiah 9:17

Obey the Word of God. If you hear only and do not act, you are only fooling yourself.

James 1:22

"Do not remember the things that have happened before. Do not think about the things of the past."

Isaiah 43:18

"I will forgive their sins. I will remember their sins no more."

Jeremiah 31:34

[God], Do not remember my sins from when I was young, or my sinful ways. By Your loving-kindness remember me for You are good, O Lord.

PSALM 25:7

Do your best to know that God is pleased with you. Be as a workman who has nothing to be ashamed of.

2 TIMOTHY 2:15

For all men have sinned and have missed the shining-greatness of God.

ROMANS 3:23

The Lord holds up all who fall. He raises up all who are brought down.

PSALM 145:14

Do not be foolish. Understand what the Lord wants you to do.

EPHESIANS 5:17

I messed up big-time, God. I had a decision to make, and I chose wrong. Now I'm beating myself up over it. . .and I'm not sure how to make it right.

I know You don't want me to be so hard on myself. Everyone makes mistakes. But I wish I had made a better choice. I'm glad that You understand me and are so forgiving. Will You help me to learn from this mistake so I won't repeat it? Give me wisdom to make good decisions. I'm young and still learning, God. Please guide me so I know right from wrong. I want to grow up making good choices—the kind that please You. I love You. Amen.

I FEEL SAD.

It's hard NOT to feel sad. Everywhere you look, you see bad things happening in the world. Add to that hard stuff going on in your own life—at home, at school, in your relationships . . .and what's a kid to do?

You might feel sad when you think about someone you love. Or, maybe there are things about yourself that make you sad.

When you're unhappy, it helps to talk with God. If you feel sad often, be sure to tell a grown-up. (Grown-ups have been around a long time, and they understand sadness. They can help.)

Always remember, God loves you. And His Word is filled with good news to turn your sadness into joy. You just need to know where to find it. The Bible verses on the following pages can help!

"This is what the Lord, the God of your father David, says, 'I have heard your prayer. I have seen your tears. See, I will heal you.' "

2 Kings 20:5

He heals those who have a broken heart. He heals their sorrows.

Psalm 147:3

Those who plant with tears will gather fruit with songs of joy.

Psalm 126:5

The Lord God will dry tears from all faces. He will take away the shame of His people from all the earth. For the Lord has spoken.

Isaiah 25:8

We give thanks to the God and Father of our Lord Jesus Christ. He is our Father Who shows us loving-kindness and our God Who gives us comfort.

2 Corinthians 1:3

My eye has grown weak with sorrow. It has grown old because of all who hate me. Go away from me, all you who sin. For the Lord has heard the sound of my crying. The Lord has heard my cry for help.

Psalm 6:7–9

"God will take away all their tears. There will be no more death or sorrow or crying or pain. All the old things have passed away."

Revelation 21:4

You will have sorrow, but your sorrow will turn into joy.

John 16:20

There is a time to cry, and a time to laugh; a time to have sorrow, and a time to dance.

Ecclesiastes 3:4

Those who have sorrow are happy, because they will be comforted.

Matthew 5:4

"Have I not told you? Be strong and have strength of heart! Do not be afraid or lose faith. For the Lord your God is with you anywhere you go."

Joshua 1:9

He gives us comfort in all our troubles. Then we can comfort other people who have the same troubles. We give the same kind of comfort God gives us.

2 Corinthians 1:4

"Peace I leave with you. My peace I give to you. I do not give peace to you as the world gives. Do not let your hearts be troubled or afraid."

John 14:27

For I know that nothing can keep us from the love of God. Death cannot! Life cannot! Angels cannot! Leaders cannot! Any other power cannot! Hard things now or in the future cannot!

Romans 8:38

"He puts those who are in low places up to high places. Those who are filled with sorrow are lifted to where they are safe."

JOB 5:11

Those who are right with the Lord cry, and He hears them. And He takes them from all their troubles.

PSALM 34:17

The Lord is near to those who have a broken heart. And He saves those who are broken in spirit.

PSALM 34:18

A man who does what is right and good may have many troubles. But the Lord takes him out of them all.

PSALM 34:19

Crying may last for a night, but joy comes with the new day.

PSALM 30:5

"In my trouble I called upon the Lord. Yes, I cried to my God. From His house He heard my voice. My cry for help came into His ears."

2 Samuel 22:7

You will keep the man in perfect peace whose mind is kept on You, because he trusts in You.

Isaiah 26:3

Why are you sad, O my soul? Why have you become troubled within me? Hope in God, for I will praise Him again for His help of being near me.

Psalm 42:5

My soul is quiet and waits for God alone. My hope comes from Him.

Psalm 62:5

Give all your worries to Him because He cares for you.

1 Peter 5:7

Since God is for us, who can be against us?

ROMANS 8:31

God loves you and has chosen you to be set apart for Himself. May God our Father and the Lord Jesus Christ give you His loving-favor and peace.

ROMANS 1:7

"He will yet make you laugh and call out with joy. Those who hate you will be dressed with shame."

JOB 8:21–22

I will be glad and full of joy in Your loving-kindness. For You have seen my suffering. You have known the troubles of my soul.

PSALM 31:7

Our Lord Jesus Christ and God our Father loves us. Through His loving-favor He gives us comfort and hope that lasts forever.

2 THESSALONIANS 2:16

Dear God, sometimes I just feel so sad. You know the reasons I feel this way. . .even when I don't quite understand why myself.

I really, really dislike this "down" feeling. I just want to be happy and have fun. And I do most of the time, but then something happens and all I want to do is cry. God, help me to see the good stuff around me and the good in people too. When I get depressed and don't feel like doing anything, remind me to pick myself up and remember that You love me. I know You will take my sadness away. I trust You, and I thank You for all the good things in my life. Amen.

I DON'T LIKE HOMEWORK!

You had fun plans for this evening or weekend, and your teachers assigned a ton of homework! What should you do? You really, *really* dislike homework after all.

You have options. 1: You could just forget about homework and do what you want—but where would that get you? Or 2: You could put on a good attitude, get the work done (your best work), and maybe even have time for some fun too.

It's all about setting priorities, staying focused, and remembering that when you work, it's just as if you are working for God Himself. So get busy! Do your best work and make God proud.

This is what the Bible has to say about it. . .

Whatever work you do, do it with all your heart. Do it for the Lord and not for men.

COLOSSIANS 3:23

Do not be lazy but always work hard. Work for the Lord with a heart full of love for Him.

ROMANS 12:11

You should work for Him without other things taking your time.

1 CORINTHIANS 7:35

Those who have sorrow should keep on working as if they had no sorrow. Those who have joy should keep on working as if there was no time for joy.

1 CORINTHIANS 7:30

Do not allow anyone to change your mind. Always do your work well for the Lord. You know that whatever you do for Him will not be wasted.

1 CORINTHIANS 15:58

Go to the ant, O lazy person. Watch and think about her ways, and be wise. She has no leader, head or ruler, but she gets her food ready in the summer, and gathers her food at the right time.

PROVERBS 6:6–8

"Love the Lord your God. Work for Him with all your heart and soul."

DEUTERONOMY 11:13

There are different kinds of work to be done for Him. But the work is for the same Lord.

1 CORINTHIANS 12:5

There are different ways of doing His work. But it is the same God who uses all these ways in all people.

1 CORINTHIANS 12:6

I have reason to be proud of my work for God. It is because I belong to Christ Jesus.

ROMANS 15:17

When men are lazy, the roof begins to fall in.
When they will do no work, the rain comes
into the house.

ECCLESIASTES 10:18

Be happy as you work. Do your work as for
the Lord, not for men.

EPHESIANS 6:7

"God will judge both the man who is right
and good, and the sinful man." For there is a
time for everything to be done and a time for
every work.

ECCLESIASTES 3:17

The hand of those who do their best will rule,
but the lazy hand will be made to work.

PROVERBS 12:24

The little troubles we suffer now for a short
time are making us ready for the great things
God is going to give us forever.

2 CORINTHIANS 4:17

Do you see a man who is good at his work? He will stand in front of kings. He will not stand in front of men who are not important.

PROVERBS 22:29

The soul of the lazy person has strong desires but gets nothing, but the soul of the one who does his best gets more than he needs.

PROVERBS 13:4

Do not be lazy. Be like those who have faith and have not given up. They will receive what God has promised them.

HEBREWS 6:12

Whatever your hand finds to do, do it with all your strength.

ECCLESIASTES 9:10

Trust your work to the Lord, and your plans will work out well.

PROVERBS 16:3

You put off the day of trouble, and bring near the seat of anger.

Amos 6:3

Our people must learn to work hard. They must work for what they need and be able to give to others who need help. Then their lives will not be wasted.

Titus 3:14

If you know what is right to do but you do not do it, you sin.

James 4:17

"Do not let your heart be troubled. You have put your trust in God, put your trust in Me also."

John 14:1

Give all your cares to the Lord and He will give you strength. He will never let those who are right with Him be shaken.

Psalm 55:22

"Come to Me, all of you who work and have heavy loads. I will give you rest."

MATTHEW 11:28

"I will forget my complaining. I will put off my sad face and be happy."

JOB 9:27

The fear of the Lord is the beginning of much learning. Fools hate wisdom and teaching.

PROVERBS 1:7

When my worry is great within me, Your comfort brings joy to my soul.

PSALM 94:19

I will show you and teach you in the way you should go. I will tell you what to do with My eye upon you.

PSALM 32:8

God, I really don't like homework. I have a teacher who gives lots of it—and I don't want to do it! I'd rather go home and relax or have fun with my friends.

I know that I need to get my homework done. If I don't, then I'll have consequences I don't want to face. I need Your help. I want to get rid of this resentful feeling. I don't want to rush through my assignments just to get them finished. I really want to do my best. Please give me the right attitude. Will You help me remember that I'm working for You? Thank You, God. Amen.

I'M SICK OF DOING CHORES.

"Work. . .work. . .work. Sometimes I feel that's all I ever do."

Have you ever said that to your parent or even yourself?

You have homework, and maybe you do volunteer work. And then you have chores at home—setting the table, doing dishes, helping to care for younger siblings and pets, keeping your room tidy, working with your family on big projects like cleaning the basement or garage. . .

The list seems endless. No wonder you're sick of chores! Still, they need to be done. Imagine if everyone decided not to do them. Soon, we'd all live in a dirty, disorganized, messed-up world.

Let's dig into God's Word and see what it says about work!

All the work he began in the house of God, obeying the Laws and looking to his God, he did with all his heart and all went well for him.

2 CHRONICLES 31:21

This work is being done with much care and is going well in their hands.

EZRA 5:8

"Yet I will have them take care of the house and do all the work that is needed to be done in it."

EZEKIEL 44:14

For we work together with God.

1 CORINTHIANS 3:9

If a man lives a clean life, he will be like a dish made of gold. He will be respected and set apart for good use by the owner of the house.

2 TIMOTHY 2:21

Clean the inside of the cup and plate, then the outside will be clean also.

MATTHEW 23:26

"Go now and work."

EXODUS 5:18

"He will have the walls and floors of the house cleaned inside."

LEVITICUS 14:41

Get your work done outside.

PROVERBS 24:27

"Make yourselves clean and change your clothes."

GENESIS 35:2

We are His work. He has made us to belong to Christ Jesus so we can work for Him. He planned that we should do this.

EPHESIANS 2:10

Give much to him, without being sorry that you do. Because the Lord your God will bring good to you for this, in all your work and in everything you do.

DEUTERONOMY 15:10

Those who wash their clothes clean are happy.

REVELATION 22:14

Then the Lord God took the man and put him in the garden of Eden to work the ground and care for it.

GENESIS 2:15

"But the seventh day is a Day of Rest to the Lord your God. You. . .must not do any work on this day."

EXODUS 20:10

And the Lord your God will bring much good upon all the work you do.

DEUTERONOMY 30:9

"Love the Lord your God. Walk in all His ways. Obey His Laws. Stay close to Him, and work for Him with all your heart and soul."

JOSHUA 22:5

That servant is happy who is doing his work when the owner comes.

LUKE 12:43

"The Father Who lives in Me does His work through Me."

JOHN 14:10

They were each given their work and load to carry, as the Lord told them to do through Moses.

NUMBERS 4:49

They brought barley and straw for the fast horses and the war-wagon horses, where it was needed. Each man did the work he had been given to do.

1 KINGS 4:28

"Come with me and see how glad I am to work for the Lord."

2 Kings 10:16

And they took their places for their work at the right times.

1 Chronicles 6:32

"I belong to God and I work for Him."

Acts 27:23

"So get ready and work, and may the Lord be with you."

1 Chronicles 22:16

They drew names for their work, the young and old alike.

1 Chronicles 25:8

Jesus said to them, "My Father is still work-ing all the time so I am working also."

John 5:17

"Six days you will do all your work."

Exodus 20:9

May the Lord reward you for your work.

Ruth 2:12

Do not work only for your own good. Think of what you can do for others.

1 Corinthians 10:24

Dear God, I want to tell You the truth: I don't like doing chores. And when I'm asked, "Did you get your work done?". . . If I'm being completely honest, I want to run the other way.

I know that doing chores is necessary, and I want to be the sort of kid who does them without complaining. But I need You to help me with that. When I want to whine and grumble, will You please speak to my heart and remind me to work willingly? If I just dig in and get things done, it won't take long at all. Then I'll feel good about what I've accomplished—and I know You will too! Thank You, God. Amen.

I'M GRUMPY!

You're grumpy! That's right. You have a bad attitude. And what's worse—you might not even know why.

We all feel grumpy sometimes. Certain things can trigger grumpiness. But often we feel that way for no good reason. It's human nature. In fact, it goes beyond being human. Look around and you'll see that animals get grumpy too. The really bad thing about grumpiness is that it's contagious. You can pass it on to your brother, sister, mom, or dad. Then, before you know it, your whole family is grumpy!

Do you want to hold on to your grumpiness, or would you rather turn your frown upside down?

Let's see what the Bible says about attitude. . .

Love does not do the wrong thing. Love never thinks of itself. Love does not get angry.

1 CORINTHIANS 13:5

Love is kind. Love is not jealous. Love does not put itself up as being important. Love has no pride.

1 CORINTHIANS 13:4

I am made happy by Your Word, like one who finds great riches.

PSALM 119:162

Have nothing to do with your old sinful life. It was sinful because of being fooled into following bad desires.

EPHESIANS 4:22

"Will not your face be happy if you do well? If you do not do well, sin is waiting to destroy you. Its desire is to rule over you, but you must rule over it."

GENESIS 4:7

Let your minds and hearts be made new.

EPHESIANS 4:23

"My heart is happy in the Lord. My strength is honored in the Lord."

1 SAMUEL 2:1

For You will make those happy who do what is right, O Lord. You will cover them all around with Your favor.

PSALM 5:12

Think as Christ Jesus thought.

PHILIPPIANS 2:5

If I make you sad, who is going to make me happy? How can you make me happy if I make you sad?

2 CORINTHIANS 2:2

God wants you to live in peace.

1 CORINTHIANS 7:15

The man who shows loving-kindness does himself good, but the man without pity hurts himself.

Proverbs 11:17

As much as you can, live in peace with all men.

Romans 12:18

Those who show loving-kindness are happy, because they will have loving-kindness shown to them.

Matthew 5:7

Anyone who shows no loving-kindness will have no loving-kindness shown to him when he is told he is guilty. But if you show loving-kindness, God will show loving-kindness to you when you are told you are guilty.

James 2:13

Work to get along with others. Live in peace.

2 Corinthians 13:11

"Because he thought he never had enough, he has nothing that gives him joy."

JOB 20:20

But the fruit that comes from having the Holy Spirit in our lives is: love, joy, peace, not giving up, being kind, being good, having faith, being gentle, and being the boss over our own desires.

GALATIANS 5:22–23

How can that which is good get along with that which is bad? How can light be in the same place with darkness?

2 CORINTHIANS 6:14

Nothing should be done because of pride or thinking about yourself. Think of other people as more important than yourself.

PHILIPPIANS 2:3

For as he thinks in his heart, so is he.

PROVERBS 23:7

Do not let kindness and truth leave you. Tie them around your neck. Write them upon your heart.

Proverbs 3:3

Help each other. Speak day after day to each other while it is still today so your heart will not become hard by being fooled by sin.

Hebrews 3:13

When what is right and fair is done, it is a joy for those who are right with God.

Proverbs 21:15

"If you want joy in your life and have happy days, keep your tongue from saying bad things and your lips from talking bad about others."

1 Peter 3:10

"I hold on to what is right and good and will not let it go."

Job 27:6

Let the words of my mouth and the thoughts of my heart be pleasing in Your eyes, O Lord, my Rock and the One Who saves me.

PSALM 19:14

Be full of joy all the time.

1 THESSALONIANS 5:16

Make a clean heart in me, O God. Give me a new spirit that will not be moved.

PSALM 51:10

The heart knows when it is bitter, and a stranger cannot share its joy.

PROVERBS 14:10

I'm having a bad day, God. I woke up feeling grumpy, and ever since, I've been stuck with a horrible attitude. What's worse is I'm passing it on to others.

I don't even know what's wrong. I just want everyone to leave me alone. Feeling like this makes me and everyone around me unhappy. So I'm trying to turn this feeling upside down. I'm working to concentrate on what's good. Your blessings are all around me, if only I try to see them. Forgive me, God, for my grumpiness, and please help to put a smile on my face. Thank You for loving me all the time—even when my attitude stinks. Amen.

NO ONE UNDERSTANDS ME.

Grown-ups think they have all the answers, you think. *They don't "get" how I feel!*

"You'll understand when you're older." You've probably heard that more times than you care to. . .but, the thing is, there's some truth in it. You can't argue that grown-ups have been around for a while. Those extra years on earth have taught them a lot. They've made mistakes—and plenty of them. Because they love you, your mom, dad, grandparents, and others don't want you to make those same mistakes. They want you to be wiser than they were at your age.

Remember: no matter how you feel, there is One who understands you *all the time*. God! His Word will make you wise if you spend time reading it and then do what it says.

Turn the page for more wisdom from God's Word.

Respect your father and mother. This is the first Law given that had a promise.

Ephesians 6:2

They give wisdom to the child-like, and much learning and wisdom to those who are young.

Proverbs 1:4

A wise man will hear and grow in learning.

Proverbs 1:5

They would not listen when I told them what they should do. They laughed at all my strong words.

Proverbs 1:30

Whoever is wise, let him understand these things and know them. For the ways of the Lord are right, and those who are right and good will follow them, but sinners will not follow them.

Hosea 14:9

"But he who listens to me will live free from danger, and he will rest easy from the fear of what is sinful."

PROVERBS 1:33

Good thinking will keep you safe. Understanding will watch over you.

PROVERBS 2:11

Fighting comes only from pride, but wisdom is with those who listen when told what they should do.

PROVERBS 13:10

The beginning of wisdom is: Get wisdom! And with all you have gotten, get understanding.

PROVERBS 4:7

Be wise in the way you live around those who are not Christians. Make good use of your time.

COLOSSIANS 4:5

The Lord built the earth by wisdom. He built the heavens by understanding.

PROVERBS 3:19

When a wise man argues with a foolish man, the fool only gets angry or laughs, and there is no peace and quiet.

PROVERBS 29:9

The Law of the Lord is perfect, giving new strength to the soul. The Law He has made known is sure, making the child-like wise.

PSALM 19:7

A fool turns away from the strong teaching of his father, but he who remembers the strong words spoken to him is wise.

PROVERBS 15:5

A wise man's heart leads him toward the right. But the foolish man's heart leads him toward the left.

ECCLESIASTES 10:2

Make your ear open to wisdom. Turn your heart to understanding.

PROVERBS 2:2

The one who is easy to fool believes everything, but the wise man looks where he goes.

PROVERBS 14:15

A fool always loses his temper, but a wise man keeps quiet.

PROVERBS 29:11

We are to be wise and to be right with God. We are to live God-like lives in this world.

TITUS 2:12

The one who talks much will for sure sin, but he who is careful what he says is wise.

PROVERBS 10:19

"God knows your hearts."

LUKE 16:15

"Wisdom is with old men, and understanding with long life."

JOB 12:12

God has looked down from heaven at the children of men to see if there is anyone who understands and looks for God.

PSALM 53:2

"It is bad for the children who will not obey!" says the Lord. "They act on a plan that is not Mine, and make an agreement that is not of My Spirit, and so add sin to sin."

ISAIAH 30:1

My children, let no one lead you in the wrong way.

1 JOHN 3:7

Be like children who obey. Do not desire to sin like you used to when you did not know any better.

1 PETER 1:14

Because Jesus was tempted as we are and suffered as we do, He understands us and He is able to help us when we are tempted.

HEBREWS 2:18

O Lord, You have looked through me and have known me.

PSALM 139:1

Now that which we see is as if we were look-ing in a broken mirror. But then we will see everything. Now I know only a part. But then I will know everything in a perfect way. That is how God knows me right now.

1 CORINTHIANS 13:12

"For the Lord looks into all hearts, and un-derstands every plan and thought."

1 CHRONICLES 28:9

Dear God, first of all, thank You for understanding me, especially when it seems like nobody else does. I know You love me, and that means a lot. I trust that You want me to do what's right and good.

I feel frustrated when grown-ups don't get how I feel. I admit, sometimes I think I know more than they do. But Your Word says that's not so. You put loving adults in my life to teach me. So, God, I promise to do my best to listen to their advice and do what they say, even when I might not understand. Amen.

IT'S NOT FAIR!

It doesn't seem fair when your older sibling gets to do something—and then your parents say you can't because you're too young. And it doesn't seem fair when your friends' parents say yes to something—and then your parents say no. It's not fair when your soccer match gets canceled because of crummy weather, or when you get sick on your birthday. . .

Truth is, the world is full of not-fair stuff. Little stuff. Big stuff. Stuff that might cause you to doubt that God knows what He's doing, or even doubt that He exists. That's why holding tight to faith and hope are so important.

The Bible says that whatever happens, we should hope things will get better and have faith that God is in control. Read the following verses from His Word. . .

"I have told you these things so you may have peace in Me. In the world you will have much trouble. But take hope! I have power over the world!"

John 16:33

"The hope of the man without God is destroyed."

Job 8:13

"If you set your heart right, and put out your hands to Him. . . . Then you would trust, because there is hope. You would look around and rest and be safe."

Job 11:13, 18

But as for me, I will always have hope and I will praise You more and more.

Psalm 71:14

For You are my hope, O Lord God. You are my trust since I was young.

Psalm 71:5

I would have been without hope if I had not believed that I would see the loving-kindness of the Lord in the land of the living.

PSALM 27:13

"For there is hope for a tree, when it is cut down, that it will grow again, and that its branches will not stop growing."

JOB 14:7

Hope that is put off makes the heart sick.

PROVERBS 13:12

So the Lord wants to show you kindness. He waits on high to have loving-pity on you. For the Lord is a God of what is right and fair. And good will come to all those who hope in Him.

ISAIAH 30:18

"Good will come to the man who trusts in the Lord, and whose hope is in the Lord."

JEREMIAH 17:7

You are as right and good as mountains are big. You are as fair when You judge as a sea is deep. O Lord, You keep safe both man and animal.

Psalm 36:6

"If it is a question of power, see, He [God] is the strong one! If it is a question of what is right and fair, who can call Him to a trial?"

Job 9:19

"For My thoughts are not your thoughts, and My ways are not your ways," says the Lord.

Isaiah 55:8

Can we say that God is not fair? No, not at all!

Romans 9:14

The Lord said, "If your faith was as a mustard seed, you could say to this tree, 'Be pulled out of the ground and planted in the sea,' and it would obey you."

Luke 17:6

" 'For I know the plans I have for you,' says the Lord, 'plans for well-being and not for trouble, to give you a future and a hope.' "

JEREMIAH 29:11

Even if the fig tree does not grow figs and there is no fruit on the vines, even if the olives do not grow and the fields give no food, even if there are no sheep within the fence and no cattle in the cattle-building, yet I will have joy in the Lord. I will be glad in the God Who saves me.

HABAKKUK 3:17–18

For the Lord loves what is fair and right. He does not leave the people alone who belong to Him.

PSALM 37:28

You know about all the troubles and hard times I have had. You have seen how I suffered. . . . Yet the Lord brought me out of all those troubles.

2 TIMOTHY 3:11

He does not want to cause trouble or sorrow for the children of men.

LAMENTATIONS 3:33

He will make good come to those who fear the Lord, both the small and the great.

PSALM 115:13

Now faith is being sure we will get what we hope for. It is being sure of what we cannot see.

HEBREWS 11:1

Then Jesus turned around. He saw her and said, "Daughter, take hope! Your faith has healed you." At once the woman was healed.

MATTHEW 9:22

Both of us need help. I can help make your faith strong and you can do the same for me. We need each other.

ROMANS 1:12

"Lord, I have faith. Help my weak faith to be stronger!"

MARK 9:24

The Lord has remembered us and will make good come to us.

PSALM 115:12

God, I'm feeling a little guilty right now because I've complained when little stuff in life didn't seem fair. And when bad stuff has happened in the world—REALLY big stuff—I've wondered if You even exist, and if You do, then why You allow such bad things to happen.

I need help with my faith. It's hard sometimes. The next time life doesn't seem fair, will You remind me of these Bible verses I've learned? Help me to remember that Your reasons are good all the time and WAY beyond my understanding. I will do my best, God, to trust that You always know what You are doing. Amen.

MY BROTHER (OR SISTER) IS BEING MEAN.

Brothers and sisters. Sometimes you like them ...sometimes you don't. It can be a challenge living together 24-7. Sometimes your sister or brother will get on your nerves. He or she might say hurtful things to or about you or do something you think is unkind or unfair.

Most of the time, though, your siblings don't truly mean those rotten things they say or do. Little disagreements are normal in a family. Still, God wants you to do your best to get along. He put you and your brother or sister in the same family for a reason—to love one another!

Let's see what the Bible says!

" 'Do not make sinful plans against one another in your hearts. And do not love to make false promises. For I hate all these things,' says the Lord."

Zechariah 8:17

See, how good and how pleasing it is for brothers to live together as one!

Psalm 133:1

"For you have taken things from your brothers when they did not owe you anything."

Job 22:6

Every one helps each other, and says to his brother, "Be strong!"

Isaiah 41:6

Why do you try to say your Christian brother is right or wrong? Why do you hate your Christian brother? We will all stand before God to be judged by Him.

Romans 14:10

Do not look down on your brother in the day of his trouble.

Obadiah 1:12

Keep on loving each other as Christian brothers.

Hebrews 13:1

"If your brother sins against you, go and tell him what he did without other people hearing it. If he listens to you, you have won your brother back again."

Matthew 18:15

A brother who has been hurt in his spirit is harder to be won than a strong city, and arguing is like the iron gates of a king's house.

Proverbs 18:19

"Do not keep from doing what is right and fair in trying to help a poor brother when he has a problem."

Exodus 23:6

Christian brothers, I ask you with all my heart in the name of the Lord Jesus Christ to agree among yourselves. Do not be divided into little groups. Think and act as if you all had the same mind.

1 Corinthians 1:10

"Say to your brothers, 'My people,' and to your sisters, 'My loved one.' "

Hosea 2:1

May all the Christian brothers have peace and love with faith from God the Father and the Lord Jesus Christ.

Ephesians 6:23

God has taught you to love each other.

1 Thessalonians 4:9

No man should do wrong to his Christian brother in anything. The Lord will punish a person who does. I have told you this before.

1 Thessalonians 4:6

Share what you have with Christian brothers who are in need.

ROMANS 12:13

Do for other people what you would like to have them do for you.

LUKE 6:31

Anyone who does not take care of his family and those in his house has turned away from the faith. He is worse than a person who has never put his trust in Christ.

1 TIMOTHY 5:8

My Christian brothers, you know everyone should listen much and speak little. He should be slow to become angry.

JAMES 1:19

Do not complain about each other, Christian brothers. Then you will not be judged. See! The Judge is standing at the door.

JAMES 5:9

Christian brothers, do not talk against anyone or speak bad things about each other. If a person says bad things about his brother, he is speaking against him. And he will be speaking against God's Law.

James 4:11

Whoever hates his brother is not in the light but lives in darkness. He does not know where he is going because the darkness has blinded his eyes.

1 John 2:11

The person who does not keep on doing what is right and does not love his brother does not belong to God.

1 John 3:10

Then Peter came to Jesus and said, "Lord, how many times may my brother sin against me and I forgive him, up to seven times?" Jesus said to him, "I tell you, not seven times but seventy times seven!"

Matthew 18:21–22

If a person says, "I love God," but hates his brother, he is a liar. If a person does not love his brother whom he has seen, how can he love God Whom he has not seen?

1 John 4:20

We have these words from Him. If you love God, love your brother also.

1 John 4:21

"If you take your gift to the altar and remember your brother has something against you, leave your gift on the altar. Go and make right what is wrong between you and him. Then come back and give your gift."

Matthew 5:23–24

Love each other with a kind heart and with a mind that has no pride.

1 Peter 3:8

Live in peace with each other.

Romans 12:16

Dear God, thank You for sisters and brothers. I do love my siblings, and no matter what, I will always be there for them. We're going to be together for the rest of our lives, and I don't want to mess that up.

Sometimes we say and do stuff that hurts each other's feelings. I'm sorry for my part in that. I'll do my best to be more patient, kind, and helpful. I want to be a good example for them, and I want to show them that I love them.

Will you lead me, God, to be the best sibling I can be? Amen.

MOM (OR DAD) SAID, "NO!"

How do you react when you want something, and Mom or Dad says no?

The key to getting along with parents is knowing that their brains are wired differently than yours. When they were kids, they thought like kids. But, over time, they matured and learned, and now they think like adults.

And they often have good reasons for saying no to your request—like maybe you aren't old enough or responsible enough to do something. Or maybe what you want to do doesn't fit with what they *have* to do. Your parents might say yes more often if you prove you're trustworthy and show that you know they want only what's best for you.

What does God's Word say about it? Read on to find out!

"Honor your father and your mother, as the Lord your God has told you. So your life may be long and it may go well with you in the land the Lord your God gives you."

DEUTERONOMY 5:16

They give wisdom to the child-like, and much learning and wisdom to those who are young.

PROVERBS 1:4

They show you how to know wisdom and teaching, to find the words of understanding.

PROVERBS 1:2

O child-like ones, learn to use wisdom.

PROVERBS 8:5

When I was a child, I spoke like a child. I thought like a child. I understood like a child. Now I am a man. I do not act like a child anymore.

1 CORINTHIANS 13:11

The Lord takes care of the child-like.

PSALM 116:6

"For God said, 'Show respect to your father and mother.' "

MATTHEW 15:4

But [God] I have trusted in Your loving-kindness. My heart will be full of joy because You will save me.

PSALM 13:5

Respect your father and mother. This is the first Law given that had a promise. The promise is this: If you respect your father and mother, you will live a long time and your life will be full of many good things.

EPHESIANS 6:2–3

But Moses said, "Why now do you sin against the Word of the Lord? It will not get you what you want."

NUMBERS 14:41

If. . .you have planned wrong-doing, put your hand on your mouth.

Proverbs 30:32

I did not know it was sin to follow wrong desires, but the Law said, "You must not follow wrong desires."

Romans 7:7

A heart that has peace is life to the body, but wrong desires are like the wasting away of the bones.

Proverbs 14:30

"Trust in the Lord your God, and you will be made strong. Trust in the men who speak for Him, and you will do well."

2 Chronicles 20:20

Then he told them what they must do. He said, "Do this in the fear of the Lord. Be faithful, and do your duty with your whole heart."

2 Chronicles 19:9

He that is faithful with little things is faithful with big things also.

Luke 16:10

"Moses said, 'Respect your father and mother.' "

Mark 7:10

God knows our desires.

2 Corinthians 4:2

Be happy in the Lord. And He will give you the desires of your heart.

Psalm 37:4

Give me understanding. Then I will listen to Your Word and obey it with all my heart.

Psalm 119:34

Think about these things and the Lord will help you understand them.

2 Timothy 2:7

What starts wars and fights among you? Is it not because you want many things and are fighting to have them?

JAMES 4:1

"Will you say what I decide is wrong? Will you say that I have done wrong, that you may be made right?"

JOB 40:8

We pray that our God will make you worth being chosen. We pray that His power will help you do the good things you want to do.

2 THESSALONIANS 1:11

Watch yourselves! You do not want to lose what we have worked for. You want to get what has been promised to you.

2 JOHN 8

"Do what is right and good in the eyes of the Lord. Then it will be well with you."

DEUTERONOMY 6:18

If you do ask, you do not receive because your reasons for asking are wrong. You want these things only to please yourselves.

JAMES 4:3

Obey your leaders and do what they say.

HEBREWS 13:17

The person who does not obey the leaders of the land is working against what God has done.

ROMANS 13:2

There was a time when we were foolish and did not obey. We were fooled in many ways. Strong desires held us in their power. We wanted only to please ourselves. We wanted what others had and were angry when we could not have them.

TITUS 3:3

God, the Bible says I should respect and honor my parents, but that's so hard sometimes—especially when I don't understand their reasons.

First of all, forgive me for those times when I've been disrespectful. Then please help me to accept my parents' decisions when they say no to something I want to do. Remind me to act in ways that will lead them to trust me with bigger, more grown-up, things.

I love my parents, God. I'm going to ask them today to forgive me for those times when I've not trusted their reasons and treated them with disrespect. Maybe You can help them to see that I'm growing up so they can trust me even more. Amen.

I THINK MY TEACHER DOESN'T LIKE ME.

If you think a teacher doesn't like you, look deeper to see if that's really true. Maybe your teacher just had a grumpy day. . .or, maybe you didn't follow the rules and that upset your teacher. Maybe you feel this way because you don't understand what he or she is trying to teach you.

Don't give your teacher a reason to dislike your behavior. Follow the rules, talk with him or her, ask for extra help. Get your parents involved. Tell them you and your teacher don't get along.

Remember, Jesus is the *best* teacher. Learn from Him. Try to do what He would do. That way, you'll always react toward your teacher in the right way.

These Bible verses will help. . .

I have not listened to the voice of my teachers. I have not turned my ear to those who would teach me.

PROVERBS 5:13

"See, God is honored in His power. Who is a teacher like Him?"

JOB 36:22

"A follower is not greater than his teacher."

MATTHEW 10:24

They came to [Jesus] and said, "Teacher, we know You are true. We know You are not afraid of what men think or say about You. You teach the way of God in truth."

MARK 12:14

He came to Jesus at night and said, "Teacher, we know You have come from God to teach us. No one can do these powerful works You do unless God is with Him."

JOHN 3:2

These men who were sent asked Jesus, "Teacher, we know what You say and teach is right. We know You do not show more respect to one person than to another. We know You teach the truth about God."

LUKE 20:21

They asked [Jesus], "Teacher, what are we to do?"

LUKE 3:12

"The follower is not more important than his teacher. But everyone who learns well will be like his teacher."

LUKE 6:40

They called to Him, "Jesus! Teacher! Take pity on us!"

LUKE 17:13

"You call Me Teacher and Lord. You are right because that is what I am."

JOHN 13:13

He who is taught God's Word should share the good things he has with his teacher.

GALATIANS 6:6

We ask you, Christian brothers, to respect those who work among you. The Lord has placed them over you and they are your teachers.

1 THESSALONIANS 5:12

"How you have given wise words to him who has no wisdom! How much true learning you have given!"

JOB 26:3

Day to day they speak. And night to night they show much learning.

PSALM 19:2

A man who cannot reason does not have much learning. A fool does not understand this.

PSALM 92:6

Take my teaching instead of silver. Take much learning instead of fine gold.

PROVERBS 8:10

Give teaching to a wise man and he will be even wiser. Teach a man who is right and good, and he will grow in learning.

PROVERBS 9:9

Wise men store up learning, but the foolish will be destroyed with their mouths.

PROVERBS 10:14

He who is careful in what he says has much learning, and he who has a quiet spirit is a man of understanding.

PROVERBS 17:27

"If you are pure and right and good, for sure [God] will help you. Because you are right and good He will put you back where you should be."

JOB 8:6

An understanding mind gets much learning, and the ear of the wise listens for much
learning.

PROVERBS 18:15

Open your heart to teaching, and your ears
to words of much learning.

PROVERBS 23:12

"Ask, and what you are asking for will be
given to you. Look, and what you are looking
for you will find. Knock, and the door you are
knocking on will be opened to you."

MATTHEW 7:7

For I give you good teaching. Do not turn
away from it.

PROVERBS 4:2

[Jesus said,] "Follow My teachings and learn
from Me. I am gentle and do not have pride.
You will have rest for your souls."

MATTHEW 11:29

The person who thinks he knows all the answers still has a lot to learn.

1 Corinthians 8:2

Learn to do good. Look for what is right and fair.

Isaiah 1:17

A young man makes himself known by his actions and proves if his ways are pure and right.

Proverbs 20:11

Let every part of you belong to the Lord Jesus Christ. Do not allow your weak thoughts to lead you into sinful actions.

Romans 13:14

He will make your being right and good show as the light, and your wise actions as the noon day.

Psalm 37:6

Jesus, I think my teacher doesn't like me. Is that true? School isn't fun when my teacher and I don't get along. . . .

Maybe if I learn to act more like You, my relationship with my teacher will get better. Will You help me? Show me what I can do. I promise to do my best to act with respect toward my teacher. If I need extra help, I won't be afraid to ask for it. I'm going to look for good things about my teacher too. Maybe that will help me to like her (or him) more. I know YOU like me, Jesus—and that means everything to me! I like You too. Amen.

I'M HAVING A HARD TIME MAKING FRIENDS.

Everyone wants a friend. Maybe you think you don't have one right now. . .but you're WRONG. You *do* have a friend. Jesus! And He's the best friend you will ever have—today and always. You can even pray and ask Jesus to help you make some new friends.

First things first: shake off any shyness. Then join in the fun! Find kids you have something in common with and invite them to hang out with you. Church is a great place to find new friends. If you like sports, joining a team is another avenue to friendship. But the best way to find friends is to act in a friendly way toward all the kids you meet.

Let's check out what God's Word has to say!

"My friends make fun of me. My eyes pour out tears to God."

Job 16:20

"Have pity on me. Have pity on me, O you my friends."

Job 19:21

"Kindness from a friend should be shown to a man without hope."

Job 6:14

Jonathan said to David, "Go in peace. For we have promised each other in the name of the Lord, saying, 'The Lord will be between me and you, and between my children and your children forever.' "

1 Samuel 20:42

Now when Job's three friends heard of all this trouble that had come upon him, they came each from his own place.

Job 2:11

Dear friend, you are doing a good work by being kind to the Christians, and for sure, to the strangers.

3 John 5

Do not let anyone fool you. Bad people can make those who want to live good become bad.

1 Corinthians 15:33

"May the Lord watch between you and me when we are apart from each other."

Genesis 31:49

"So come now, let us meet to speak with each other."

Nehemiah 6:7

There are many people who belong to Christ. And yet, we are one body which is Christ's. We are all different but we depend on each other.

Romans 12:5

"They are joined one to another. They hold on to each other and cannot be separated."

Job 41:17

Loving-kindness and truth have met together.

Psalm 85:10

Try to understand other people. Forgive each other. If you have something against someone, forgive him. That is the way the Lord forgave you.

Colossians 3:13

Help each other in troubles and problems. This is the kind of law Christ asks us to obey.

Galatians 6:2

You must be kind to each other. Think of the other person. Forgive other people just as God forgave you because of Christ's death on the cross.

Ephesians 4:32

Be willing to help and care for each other because of Christ. By doing this, you honor Christ.

EPHESIANS 5:21

Do not lie to each other. You have put out of your life your old ways.

COLOSSIANS 3:9

May the Lord make you grow in love for each other and for everyone.

1 THESSALONIANS 3:12

Do not let anyone pay back for the bad he received. But look for ways to do good to each other and to all people.

1 THESSALONIANS 5:15

Talk once or twice to a person who tries to divide people into groups against each other. If he does not stop, have nothing to do with him.

TITUS 3:10

Remember to do good and help each other. Gifts like this please God.

HEBREWS 13:16

"For where two or three are gathered together in My name, there I am with them."

MATTHEW 18:20

From now on you are not strangers and people who are not citizens. You are citizens together with those who belong to God. You belong in God's family.

EPHESIANS 2:19

God has given each of you a gift. Use it to help each other. This will show God's loving-favor.

1 PETER 4:10

Be gentle as you care for each other. God works against those who have pride. He gives His loving-favor to those who do not try to honor themselves.

1 PETER 5:5

God is faithful. He chose you to be joined together with His Son, Jesus Christ our Lord.

1 Corinthians 1:9

Receive each other as Christ received you. This will honor God.

Romans 15:7

May their hearts be given comfort. May they be brought close together in Christian love. May they be rich in understanding and know God's secret. It is Christ Himself.

Colossians 2:2

Dear Jesus, I'm so glad You are my friend. Talking with You and knowing You are always with me helps me to feel less lonely. I sure would like some friends my own age, though.

I have trouble meeting other kids. It's hard for me to introduce myself to someone new; instead, I wait for them to come to me, and that doesn't always work.

I'm going to try harder to get to know some new kids. Maybe You could lead me to the ones you approve of at school and other places? I'm sure there are some really good friends out there just waiting to know me! Thanks for Your help, Jesus. Amen.

I SAT ALL ALONE AT LUNCH.

There you are, sitting all alone in the lunch-room staring at your peanut butter and jelly sandwich. You imagine all eyes shifting toward you and kids whispering, "Look at that kid over there sitting alone." Your heart races. Your face turns red with embarrassment as you tell yourself: *They know! And no one cares that I'm eating alone!*

Does that sound like you? Turn off that sour thinking. Those other kids are too busy eating and talking to notice that you're by yourself. So why not take a chance? Seek out kids who seem nice, and ask if you can sit with them. What's the worst that could happen? They might say no—and nothing changes. But what if they say yes? It could be the beginning to a great friendship!

God doesn't want you to feel upset about being alone. . .after all, He's *always* with you! Here's what His Word has to say about it. . .

Then the Lord God said, "It is not good for man to be alone. I will make a helper that is right for him."

Genesis 2:18

"Be strong and have strength of heart. Do not be afraid or shake with fear because of them. For the Lord your God is the One Who goes with you. He will be faithful to you. He will not leave you alone."

Deuteronomy 31:6

Be happy to have people stay. . .and eat with you.

1 Peter 4:9

Those who know Your name will put their trust in You. For You, O Lord, have never left alone those who look for You.

Psalm 9:10

God makes a home for those who are alone.

Psalm 68:6

"No man will be able to stand against you all the days of your life. I will be with you just as I have been with Moses. I will be faithful to you and will not leave you alone."

JOSHUA 1:5

It is good when people help you if they do not hope to get something from it. They should help you all the time, not only when I am with you.

GALATIANS 4:18

What will I do when God speaks to me? When He asks me why, what will I answer Him? . . . If I have eaten my food alone without sharing it with the child who has no parents.

JOB 31:14, 17

"Do not fear, for I am with you. Do not be afraid, for I am your God. I will give you strength, and for sure I will help you. Yes, I will hold you up with My right hand that is right and good."

ISAIAH 41:10

"The Lord will not leave His people alone, because of His great name. The Lord has been pleased to make you His people."

1 Samuel 12:22

I have been young, and now I am old. Yet I have never seen the man who is right with God left alone, or his children begging for bread.

Psalm 37:25

God has said, "I will never leave you or let you be alone."

Hebrews 13:5

"I will not leave you without help as children without parents. I will come to you."

John 14:18

Of what great worth is Your loving-kindness, O God! The children of men come and are safe in the shadow of Your wings.

Psalm 36:7

Turn to me and show me Your loving-kindness. For I am alone and in trouble.

Psalm 25:16

"See, I am with you. I will care for you everywhere you go."

Genesis 28:15

O my God, I trust in You. Do not let me be ashamed. Do not let those who fight against me win.

Psalm 25:2

"Fear not, for you will not be ashamed. Do not be troubled, for you will not be put to shame. You will forget how you were ashamed when you were young."

Isaiah 54:4

"But I have prayed for you. I have prayed that your faith will be strong and that you will not give up."

Luke 22:32

"Do not be afraid of them. For I am with you to take you out of trouble," says the Lord.

JEREMIAH 1:8

Wait for the Lord. Be strong. Let your heart be strong. Yes, wait for the Lord.

PSALM 27:14

But when I would fall, they would gather together in joy. Those who say things to hurt people would gather against me. I did not know them. They spoke against me without stopping.

PSALM 35:15

"Do for other people whatever you would like to have them do for you."

MATTHEW 7:12

The trouble he makes will return to him. When he hurts others it will come down on his own head.

PSALM 7:16

He does not hurt others with his tongue, or do wrong to his neighbor, or bring shame to his friend.

PSALM 15:3

Yes, let no one who hopes in You be put to shame. But put to shame those who hurt others without a reason.

PSALM 25:3

They ground their teeth at me like bad people making fun of others at a special supper.

PSALM 35:16

Let all who are happy because of my trouble be ashamed and without honor. Let those who think they are better than I, be covered with shame and without honor.

PSALM 35:26

You have seen it, O Lord. Do not keep quiet. O Lord, do not be far from me.

PSALM 35:22

God, I've discovered from Your Word that I'm not the first one to feel left out. I also know that You will help me. You promise to stay with me all the time and make me strong.

Sometimes I want to get back at the kids who ignore me. But from now on, I'm going to trust You to handle it. I'm going to treat others like Jesus would. He said I should do for other people what I would like them to do for me. Help me with that, God—and will You send me some lunch partners too? Thank You, and amen.

I FEEL LIKE I'M NOT GOOD ENOUGH.

Do you hear a little voice inside you saying, "You're not good enough"? Maybe someone picked on you, and you felt not good enough. Or maybe there's something you'd like to do, but you feel not talented enough. . . .

That little voice inside is Satan trying to make you feel bad about *YOU*. The truth is this: you ARE good enough. Right now. Just the way you are. And God is helping you become even better. He made you, and He loves you. You are His work in progress. Every day He's making little changes in you that lead you toward excellence.

The Bible is filled with stories about people who thought they weren't good enough—until God showed them they were. Continue reading to see what God's Word has to say about the value of YOU!

For You made the parts inside me. You put me together inside my mother. I will give thanks to You, for the greatness of the way I was made. . . . Your works are great and my soul knows it very well.

PSALM 139:13–14

But now, O Lord, You are our Father. We are the clay, and You are our pot maker. All of us are the work of Your hand.

ISAIAH 64:8

"Remember that You have made me as clay. Would You turn me into dust again?"

JOB 10:9

"Your hands put me together and made me, and now would You destroy me?"

JOB 10:8

"You are of great worth in My eyes. You are honored and I love you."

ISAIAH 43:4

Your beauty should come from the inside. It should come from the heart. This is the kind that lasts. Your beauty should be a gentle and quiet spirit. In God's sight this is of great worth and no amount of money can buy it.

1 Peter 3:4

Who are you to talk back to God? A pot being made from clay does not talk to the man making it and say, "Why did you make me like this?"

Romans 9:20

Know that the Lord is God. It is He Who made us, and not we ourselves. We are His people and the sheep of His field.

Psalm 100:3

Moses said to the Lord, "Lord, I am not a man of words. I have never been. . . . For I am slow in talking and it is difficult for me to speak." Then the Lord said to him, "Who has made man's mouth? . . . Is it not I, the Lord?"

Exodus 4:10–11

You have taken me away from the fighting of the people. You have made me the leader of nations. People whom I have not known will serve me.

PSALM 18:43

I am sure that God Who began the good work in you will keep on working in you until the day Jesus Christ comes again.

PHILIPPIANS 1:6

You [God] have also given me the covering that saves me. Your right hand holds me up. And Your care has made me great.

PSALM 18:35

I will cry to God Most High, to God Who finishes all things for me.

PSALM 57:2

"I planted you as a vine of much worth, in every way a true seed."

JEREMIAH 2:21

"Look at the birds. They do not plant seeds. They do not gather grain. They have no grain buildings for keeping grain. Yet God feeds them. Are you not worth more than the birds?"

LUKE 12:24

"Are not five small birds sold for two small pieces of money? God does not forget even one of the birds. God knows how many hairs you have on your head. . . . You are worth more than many small birds."

LUKE 12:6–7

We know we are not able in ourselves to do any of this work. God makes us able to do these things.

2 CORINTHIANS 3:5

Then the Lord said to Abraham, "Why did Sarah laugh and say, 'How can I give birth to a child when I am so old?' Is anything too hard for the Lord?"

GENESIS 18:13–14

But we have power over all these things through Jesus Who loves us so much.

ROMANS 8:37

[God] answered me, "I am all you need. I give you My loving-favor. My power works best in weak people."

2 CORINTHIANS 12:9

I can do all things because Christ gives me the strength.

PHILIPPIANS 4:13

"But I am only a little child. I do not know how to start or finish."

1 KINGS 3:7

Then Peter said, "I can see, for sure, that God does not respect one person more than another. He is pleased with any man in any nation who honors Him and does what is right."

ACTS 10:34–35

I am sure that God Who began the good work in you will keep on working in you until the day Jesus Christ comes again.

PHILIPPIANS 1:6

Do not have joy over me, you who hate me. When I fall, I will rise. Even though I am in darkness, the Lord will be my light.

MICAH 7:8

You are now children of God because you have put your trust in Christ Jesus.

GALATIANS 3:26

God does not show favor to one man more than to another.

ROMANS 2:11

"There no man will be able to stand in front of you. The Lord your God will put the fear of you on all the land where you walk, as He has promised you."

DEUTERONOMY 11:25

God, I really need your help. . . .

Sometimes I don't like myself. I can't even tell You why, exactly. It's just a feeling I get. Little things add up and make me think I'm not good enough or smart enough. Some days I even wonder if I'm lovable. But, God, I know You don't want me to think that way.

You made me. You love me. The Bible is filled with words that promise You are with me and will help me—especially with stuff I think I can't do. Make me strong, God. Stop Satan from saying bad stuff about me. Please help me to love myself more, like the way You love me. Amen.

SOMEONE WANTS ME TO DO SOMETHING BAD.

Is someone pressuring you to do something you know is wrong?

It's hard to resist temptation. That little voice—the one that's NOT God—loves telling you lies. Satan wants you to do things that displease God.

Did you know that Satan even tried to get Jesus to disobey? For forty days, when Jesus was alone in the desert, the devil kept trying to trick Him into disobeying God, but Jesus didn't give in. He didn't even *think* about allowing Satan to trap Him. "Get away, Satan." Jesus said, "It is written, 'You must worship the Lord your God. You must obey Him only' " (Matthew 4:10).

You can have the courage to stand up to Satan too! God's Word will help you chase him away.

"The devil has nothing to do with the truth. There is no truth in him. It is expected of the devil to lie, for he is a liar and the father of lies."

John 8:44

God gave Jesus of Nazareth the Holy Spirit and power. He went around doing good and healing all who were troubled by the devil because God was with Him.

Acts 10:38

It is no surprise! The devil makes himself look like an angel of light.

2 Corinthians 11:14

Put on the things God gives you to fight with. Then you will not fall into the traps of the devil.

Ephesians 6:11

Do not let the devil start working in your life.

Ephesians 4:27

Wear shoes on your feet which are the Good News of peace.

Ephesians 6:15

Then Saul said, "You false preacher and trouble-maker! You son of the devil! You hate what is right! Will you always be turning people from the right ways of the Lord?"

Acts 13:10

You have kept God's Word in your hearts. You have power over the devil.

1 John 2:14

So stand up and do not be moved. Wear a belt of truth around your body. Wear a piece of iron over your chest which is being right with God.

Ephesians 6:14

The Lord is faithful. He will give you strength and keep you safe from the devil.

2 Thessalonians 3:3

We know that no child of God keeps on sinning. The Son of God watches over him and the devil cannot get near him.

1 JOHN 5:18

We know that we belong to God, but the whole world is under the power of the devil.

1 JOHN 5:19

The covering for your head is that you have been saved from the punishment of sin. Take the sword of the Spirit which is the Word of God.

EPHESIANS 6:17

Give yourselves to God. Stand against the devil and he will run away from you.

JAMES 4:7

Most important of all, you need a covering of faith in front of you. This is to put out the fire-arrows of the devil.

EPHESIANS 6:16

This is the way you can know who are the children of God and who are the children of the devil. The person who does not keep on doing what is right and does not love his brother does not belong to God.

1 JOHN 3:10

You followed the sinful ways of the world and obeyed the leader of the power of darkness. He is the devil who is now working in the people who do not obey God.

EPHESIANS 2:2

My children, let no one lead you in the wrong way. The man who does what is right, is right with God in the same way as Christ is right with God.

1 JOHN 3:7

"Be very careful what you do. For the Lord our God will have nothing to do with what is not right and good, or with what is not fair, or with taking pay for doing what is wrong."

2 CHRONICLES 19:7

To do what is right and good and fair is more pleasing to the Lord than gifts given on the altar in worship.

PROVERBS 21:3

"Do what is right and good in the eyes of the Lord. Then it will be well with you."

DEUTERONOMY 6:18

"Learn to do good. Look for what is right and fair. Speak strong words to those who make it hard for people."

ISAIAH 1:17

For You will make those happy who do what is right, O Lord. You will cover them all around with Your favor.

PSALM 5:12

A man who does what is right and good may have many troubles. But the Lord takes him out of them all.

PSALM 34:19

He. . .walks without blame and does what is right and good, and speaks the truth in his heart. He does not hurt others with his tongue, or do wrong to his neighbor, or bring shame to his friend.

PSALM 15:2–3

When someone does something bad to you, do not pay him back with something bad. Try to do what all men know is right and good.

ROMANS 12:17

Do not give any part of your body for sinful use. Instead, give yourself to God as a living person who has been raised from the dead. Give every part of your body to God to do what is right.

ROMANS 6:13

But even if you suffer for doing what is right, you will be happy. Do not be afraid or troubled by what they may do to make it hard for you.

1 PETER 3:14

Wow, God! Your Word sure has a lot to say about doing what is right and good.

Sometimes my friends want to do things that I know are wrong. When they ask me to go along with them, it's hard to say no because I want us to stay friends. God, please help me to do what I know is right—even if it means losing a friend.

I want to follow the rules and do what pleases You. Teach me to do what is right. Maybe how I act will set a good example. Then I can tell my friends about You, and they'll want to please You too! Amen.

I SAID SOMETHING I SHOULDN'T HAVE.

You did it. You spoke without first thinking about your words, and it got you into trouble. . . . You're not alone. Everyone messes up with their words sometimes.

Words have tons of power. So you need to think before you speak. If you say things that are good, right, and true, you please God. But He doesn't like it when you lie, gossip, or use bad language. Never be afraid to speak up about the truth. Use honest words. They make God happy. And do your best to speak to everyone with words that are respectful and kind.

This is what the Bible says about words. . .

Pleasing words are like honey. They are sweet to the soul and healing to the bones.

Proverbs 16:24

You have been trapped with the words of your lips. You have been caught with the words of your mouth.

Proverbs 6:2

O Lord, save me from lying lips and a false tongue.

Psalm 120:2

A man will be filled with good from the fruit of his words.

Proverbs 12:14

"Good comes from a good man because of the riches he has in his heart. Sin comes from a sinful man because of the sin he has in his heart. The mouth speaks of what the heart is full of."

Luke 6:45

There is one whose foolish words cut like a sword, but the tongue of the wise brings healing.

PROVERBS 12:18

The words of a man's mouth are deep waters. Wisdom comes like a flowing river making a pleasant noise.

PROVERBS 18:4

Like a sparrow in its traveling, like a swallow in its flying, so bad words said against someone without reason do not come to rest.

PROVERBS 26:2

An arguing man makes fights worse. He is like coals to burning wood and wood to a fire.

PROVERBS 26:21

A lying tongue hates those it crushes, and a mouth that speaks false words destroys.

PROVERBS 26:28

With our tongue we give thanks to our Father in heaven. And with our tongue we speak bad words against men who are made like God.

JAMES 3:9

"You will be guilty of the same things you find in others. When you say what is wrong in others, your words will be used to say what is wrong in you."

MATTHEW 7:2

Watch your talk! No bad words should be coming from your mouth. Say what is good. Your words should help others grow as Christians.

EPHESIANS 4:29

We all make many mistakes. If anyone does not make a mistake with his tongue by saying the wrong things, he is a perfect man. It shows he is able to make his body do what he wants it to do.

JAMES 3:2

All the words of my mouth are right and good. There is nothing in them that is against the truth.

PROVERBS 8:8

"For it is by your words that you will not be guilty and it is by your words that you will be guilty."

MATTHEW 12:37

The Lord hates lying lips, but those who speak the truth are His joy.

PROVERBS 12:22

Speak with them in such a way they will want to listen to you. Do not let your talk sound foolish. Know how to give the right answer to anyone.

COLOSSIANS 4:6

When people say bad things about us, we answer with kind words.

1 CORINTHIANS 4:13

A man who gives his neighbor sweet-sounding words that are not true spreads a net for his own feet.

PROVERBS 29:5

Do not be guilty of telling bad stories and of foolish talk. These things are not for you to do.

EPHESIANS 5:4

"Do not use the name of the Lord your God in a false way. For the Lord will punish the one who uses His name in a false way."

EXODUS 20:7

The tongue is. . .a small part of the body, but it can speak big things. See how a very small fire can set many trees on fire.

JAMES 3:5

Giving thanks and speaking bad words come from the same mouth. My Christian brothers, this is not right!

JAMES 3:10

With his mouth he swears and lies. He makes it hard for other people. Trouble and sin are under his tongue.

Psalm 10:7

He who is always telling stories makes secrets known, but he who can be trusted keeps a thing hidden.

Proverbs 11:13

One who hurts people with bad talk separates good friends.

Proverbs 16:28

He who watches over his mouth and his tongue keeps his soul from troubles.

Proverbs 21:23

"Keep these words in your heart that I am telling you today."

Deuteronomy 6:6

Dear God, please forgive me for when I've used words that You don't approve of. I'm sorry for not thinking before I speak. Sometimes when I'm angry, I say things that I don't mean. My words haven't always been kind, and sometimes they've torn people down instead of building them up.

I'm going to try harder to think before I say something that might hurt others—and especially You! I want all the words that come from my mouth to be honest, respectful, and pleasing to You. Amen.

I FEEL AFRAID.

What scares you? Loud noises. . .high places
. . .spiders. . .? Everyone has something he or
she is afraid of.

The Bible tells of a time Jesus' disciples
were afraid. They were with Jesus in a small
boat crossing the Sea of Galilee when a thun-
derstorm happened. The wind howled! Waves
rocked the boat, making the disciples fear it
would capsize. All the while, Jesus slept.

"Wake up!" the disciples shouted. "Aren't
You afraid we'll drown?"

But Jesus wasn't afraid. He had faith.

"Be still," He told the storm, and it immedi-
ately calmed down (Mark 4:35–41).

Faith is the key to being unafraid—faith
and trusting that Jesus is always with you,
helping you, no matter what.

What does the Bible say about being
afraid? Turn the page to find out!

The Lord is my light and the One Who saves me. Whom should I fear? The Lord is the strength of my life. Of whom should I be afraid?

PSALM 27:1

Yes, even if I walk through the valley of the shadow of death, I will not be afraid of anything, because You are with me. You have a walking stick with which to guide and one with which to help. These comfort me.

PSALM 23:4

So we will not be afraid, even if the earth is shaken and the mountains fall into the center of the sea.

PSALM 46:2

"Be strong and have strength of heart. Do not be afraid or shake with fear because of them. For the Lord your God is the One Who goes with you. He will be faithful to you. He will not leave you alone."

DEUTERONOMY 31:6

Even if an army gathers against me, my heart will not be afraid. Even if war rises against me, I will be sure of You.

PSALM 27:3

"Do not fear, for I am with you. Do not be afraid, for I am your God. I will give you strength, and for sure I will help you. Yes, I will hold you up with My right hand that is right and good."

ISAIAH 41:10

Do not be afraid of fear that comes all at once.

PROVERBS 3:25

[Jesus] said to His followers, "Why are you so full of fear? Do you not have faith?"

MARK 4:40

And so my heart is glad. My soul is full of joy. My body also will rest without fear.

PSALM 16:9

"Do not fear, for I am with you. I will bring your children from the east, and I will gather you from the west."

ISAIAH 43:5

There is no fear in love. Perfect love puts fear out of our hearts. People have fear when they are afraid of being punished. The man who is afraid does not have perfect love.

1 JOHN 4:18

"Listen to Me, you who know what is right and good, you people who have My Law in your hearts. Do not fear the shame of strong words from man. Do not be troubled when they speak against you."

ISAIAH 51:7

Those who do right do not have to be afraid of the leaders. Those who do wrong are afraid of them. Do you want to be free from fear of them? Then do what is right. You will be respected instead.

ROMANS 13:3

For God did not give us a spirit of fear. He gave us a spirit of power and of love and of a good mind.

2 Timothy 1:7

God is love.

1 John 4:8

"Do not fear. Do not be afraid. Have I not made it known to you from long ago? And you have heard Me. Is there a God besides Me? No, there is no other Rock. I know of none."

Isaiah 44:8

"Do not be afraid. For I have bought you and made you free. I have called you by name. You are Mine!"

Isaiah 43:1

You will not be afraid when you lie down. When you lie down, your sleep will be sweet.

Proverbs 3:24

I will not be afraid of ten thousands of people who stand all around against me.

PSALM 3:6

When I am afraid, I will trust in You.

PSALM 56:3

"When you pass through the waters, I will be with you. When you pass through the rivers, they will not flow over you. When you walk through the fire, you will not be burned. The fire will not destroy you. For I am the Lord your God, the Holy One of Israel, Who saves you."

ISAIAH 43:2–3

"The God Who lives forever is your safe place. His arms are always under you."

DEUTERONOMY 33:27

You will not be afraid of the sickness that walks in darkness, or of the trouble that destroys at noon.

PSALM 91:6

He will not be afraid of bad news. His heart is strong because he trusts in the Lord.

PSALM 112:7

In God I have put my trust. I will not be afraid. What can man do to me?

PSALM 56:11

Of what great worth is Your loving-kindness, O God! The children of men come and are safe in the shadow of Your wings.

PSALM 36:7

He will cover you with His wings. And under His wings you will be safe. He is faithful like a safe-covering and a strong wall.

PSALM 91:4

The Lord is good, a safe place in times of trouble. And He knows those who come to Him to be safe.

NAHUM 1:7

God, I need Your help because I'm scared.

Sometimes fear comes suddenly. Unexpected things happen, and they frighten me. I face what's unfamiliar, and then I get afraid that something bad could happen to me.

But the Bible says that I don't have to be afraid of anything because You love me. You are in control. You are with me—You're my all-the-time safe place whenever there's trouble.

God, I trust You. I believe that You've got it handled, whatever comes my way. So please keep me calm. Remind me that I'm safe with You today, tomorrow, and forever. Amen.

IT'S MORE THAN I CAN HANDLE!

"It's just too much! Too much homework, too much to do, too much of everything all at once. It's more than I can take right now!"

Does that sound like you? If you're like everybody else, then surely you have bad days when the world dumps on you—chores, trouble, worries. . . Everything seems to pile up around you until you feel like giving in and doing something you know is wrong or running away from your troubles.

But giving in and running aren't going to solve anything. Besides, God promises never to allow more than you can handle. When it feels like too much, His Word has just the encouragement you need to get out of the mess that clouds your day.

Let's see what the Bible says. . .

You have never been tempted to sin in any different way than other people. God is faithful. He will not allow you to be tempted more than you can take. But when you are tempted, He will make a way for you to keep from falling into sin.

1 Corinthians 10:13

"He puts those who are in low places up to high places. Those who are filled with sorrow are lifted to where they are safe."

Job 5:11

Be pleased to save me, O Lord. Hurry, O Lord, to help me.

Psalm 40:13

Let my prayer come to You. Help me because of Your Word.

Psalm 119:170

He lifted me out of many waters.

Psalm 18:16

Then she came and got down before Jesus and worshiped Him. She said, "Lord, help me!"

The Lord knows how to help men who are right with God when they are tempted.

2 PETER 2:9

"The one who is right with God will hold to his way. And he who has clean hands will become stronger and stronger."

JOB 17:9

Give all your cares to the Lord and He will give you strength. He will never let those who are right with Him be shaken.

PSALM 55:22

The man who does not give up when tests come is happy. After the test is over, he will receive the crown of life. God has promised this to those who love Him.

JAMES 1:12

He helps those who have a bad power over them.

Psalm 146:7

Moses said to the people, "Do not be afraid! Be strong, and see how the Lord will save you today."

Exodus 14:13

"You be strong. Do not lose strength of heart. For you will be paid for your work."

2 Chronicles 15:7

Be strong. Be strong in heart, all you who hope in the Lord.

Psalm 31:24

We ask you, Christian brothers, speak to those who do not want to work. Comfort those who feel they cannot keep going on. Help the weak. Understand and be willing to wait for all men.

1 Thessalonians 5:14

Every one helps each other, and says to his brother, "Be strong!"

Isaiah 41:6

Hear my prayer, O Lord. Listen when I ask for help. Answer me because You are faithful and right.

Psalm 143:1

I pray that God's great power will make you strong, and that you will have joy as you wait and do not give up.

Colossians 1:11

When we have learned not to give up, it shows we have stood the test. When we have stood the test, it gives us hope.

Romans 5:4

Be happy in your hope. Do not give up when trouble comes. Do not let anything stop you from praying.

Romans 12:12

We are glad for our troubles also. We know that troubles help us learn not to give up.

ROMANS 5:3

I did not give up waiting for the Lord. And He turned to me and heard my cry.

PSALM 40:1

Hear, O Lord. And show me loving-kindness. O Lord, be my Helper.

PSALM 30:10

Rest in the Lord and be willing to wait for Him.

PSALM 37:7

Take your share of suffering as a good soldier of Jesus Christ.

2 TIMOTHY 2:3

"What a help you are to the weak! How you have saved the arm that has no strength!"

JOB 26:2

"He gives strength to the weak. And He gives power to him who has little strength."

ISAIAH 40:29

"Come to Me, all of you who work and have heavy loads. I will give you rest."

MATTHEW 11:28

I will lift up my eyes to the mountains. Where will my help come from? My help comes from the Lord, Who made heaven and earth.

PSALM 121:1–2

But you, Christian brothers, do not get tired of doing good.

2 THESSALONIANS 3:13

God, I get so overwhelmed sometimes. There's too much going on! It's like a fight happening inside me, tugging me one way and then the other. I just want everything to stop piling up; I want life to be simple.

I know You never promise easy, but You do promise to help. So be my Helper, God. Help me to stop, take a deep breath, and tackle my problems one at a time. Give me everything I need to make wise choices and also to rest in Your love. Together, we will get through this—I know we will, with You leading the way. I love You, God, and I trust You. Amen.

I'M SICK AND TIRED OF
W-A-I-T-I-N-G!

What's taking so long? You've hoped, prayed, trusted, but nothing has happened. You wonder, *Where is God? Why does He seem so far away?*

The answer to those questions is in the Bible in 2 Peter 3:8: "Dear friends, remember this one thing, with the Lord one day is as 1,000 years, and 1,000 years are as one day."

God lives in a different time zone. Heaven time! So what seems like a long time waiting for us. . .well, it isn't long at all for Him. And that's where patience comes in. God wants us to learn patience. And while we're waiting, He wants us to continue to hope, trust, and believe that He's working on whatever we've asked Him for.

Here's what the Bible says about waiting. . .

Wait for the Lord. Be strong. Let your heart be strong. Yes, wait for the Lord.

Psalm 27:14

There is a special time for everything. There is a time for everything that happens under heaven.

Ecclesiastes 3:1

"For My thoughts are not your thoughts, and My ways are not your ways," says the Lord.

Isaiah 55:8

"For as the heavens are higher than the earth, so are My ways higher than your ways, and My thoughts than your thoughts."

Isaiah 55:9

But they who wait upon the Lord will get new strength. They will rise up with wings like eagles. They will run and not get tired. They will walk and not become weak.

Isaiah 40:31

He has made everything beautiful in its time.

ECCLESIASTES 3:11

Rest in the Lord and be willing to wait for Him.

PSALM 37:7

Do not say, "I will punish wrong-doing." Wait on the Lord, and He will take care of it.

PROVERBS 20:22

The Lord is good to those who wait for Him, to the one who looks for Him.

LAMENTATIONS 3:25

But the Lord favors those who fear Him and those who wait for His loving-kindness.

PSALM 147:11

But as for me, I will watch for the Lord. I will wait for the God Who saves me. My God will hear me.

MICAH 7:7

For it is not yet time for it to come true. . . . If you think it is slow in coming, wait for it. For it will happen for sure, and it will not wait.

HABAKKUK 2:3

But if we hope for something we do not yet see, we must learn how to wait for it.

ROMANS 8:25

He said, "It is not for you to know the special days or the special times which the Father has put in His own power."

ACTS 1:7

Abraham was willing to wait and God gave to him what He had promised.

HEBREWS 6:15

You must be willing to wait without giving up. After you have done what God wants you to do, God will give you what He promised you.

HEBREWS 10:36

Learn well how to wait so you will be strong and complete and in need of nothing.

JAMES 1:4

Learn from the farmer. He waits for the good fruit from the earth until the early and late rains come.

JAMES 5:7

The Lord is not slow about keeping His promise as some people think.

2 PETER 3:9

"The smallest one will become a family of a thousand. And the least one will become a powerful nation. I, the Lord, will make it happen in its time."

ISAIAH 60:22

For a thousand years in Your eyes are like yesterday when it passes by, or like the hours of the night.

PSALM 90:4

For there is a right time and way for every-thing, even if a man's trouble is heavy upon him.

ECCLESIASTES 8:6

You must pray at all times as the Holy Spirit leads you to pray. Pray for the things that are needed. You must watch and keep on praying.

EPHESIANS 6:18

A man cannot please God unless he has faith. Anyone who comes to God must believe that He is. That one must also know that God gives what is promised to the one who keeps on looking for Him.

HEBREWS 11:6

I did not give up waiting for the Lord. And He turned to me and heard my cry. He brought me up out of the hole of danger, out of the mud and clay. He set my feet on a rock, making my feet sure.

PSALM 40:1–2

For I hope in You, O Lord. You will answer, O Lord my God.

Psalm 38:15

I will wait for the Lord. . . . I trust Him and hope in Him.

Isaiah 8:17

I wait for the Lord. My soul waits and I hope in His Word.

Psalm 130:5

Every word of God has been proven true. He is a safe-covering to those who trust in Him.

Proverbs 30:5

At the right time, we will be shown that God is the One Who has all power. He is the King of kings and Lord of lords.

1 Timothy 6:15

God, please forgive me for not understanding Your timing. I've only thought about things as they are here on earth; I've never even considered that You measure time differently up there in heaven. So please help me to be patient with You. I trust that You hear my prayers and that You will answer the right way when the time is right.

Help me to be more patient with everyday things as well. Too often, I want stuff "right now." Thank You for teaching me to wait, God. I learn something new from You every day, and I'm grateful. Amen.

I'M WORRIED ABOUT EVERYTHING!

ANXIETY. It's that uneasy feeling that comes from not knowing—or worrying about—what's going to happen. You're nervous, edgy, jumpy—thinking about what might be lurking where you can't see it. . . .

What are you worried about today? When you feel anxious, it's important to remember all the good promises God made you—promises to love you, stay with you, and protect you; promises to help you and give you strength to handle whatever comes your way.

God always keeps His promises. So trust Him with everything that makes you anxious. God knows what's coming, and He *already* has it under control. You are His special child. He loves you, and He won't let you down. You can believe *everything* in His Word.

Let's see what God's Word has to say about worry. . .

"Do not worry about tomorrow. Tomorrow will have its own worries. The troubles we have in a day are enough for one day."

MATTHEW 6:34

"The Lord says to you, 'Do not be afraid or troubled because of these many men. For the battle is not yours but God's.'"

2 CHRONICLES 20:15

"Which of you can make himself a little taller by worrying?"

MATTHEW 6:27

Do not worry. Learn to pray about everything. Give thanks to God as you ask Him for what you need.

PHILIPPIANS 4:6

O my soul? Why have you become troubled within me? Hope in God, for I will praise Him again for His help of being near me.

PSALM 42:5

Do not worry yourself because of those who do wrong.

PROVERBS 24:19

Give all your worries to Him because He cares for you.

1 PETER 5:7

Worry in the heart of a man weighs it down.

PROVERBS 12:25

Through His shining-greatness and perfect life, He has given us promises. These promises are of great worth and no amount of money can buy them.

2 PETER 1:4

The Lord is my rock, and my safe place, and the One Who takes me out of trouble. My God is my rock, in Whom I am safe. He is my safe-covering, my saving strength, and my strong tower.

PSALM 18:2

"He. . .gives what is right and fair to those who are troubled."

JOB 36:6

"Do not let your heart be troubled. You have put your trust in God, put your trust in Me [Jesus] also."

JOHN 14:1

Do not be troubled in mind or worried by the talk you hear.

2 THESSALONIANS 2:2

"O Lord, God of Israel, there is no God like You in heaven or on earth. You keep Your promises and show loving-kindness to Your servants who walk with You with all their hearts."

2 CHRONICLES 6:14

God is greater than our heart. He knows everything.

1 JOHN 3:20

"I can see the Lord before me all the time. He is at my right side so that I do not need to be troubled."

Acts 2:25

And God said to Moses, "I AM WHO I AM."

Exodus 3:14

God cannot lie. We who have turned to Him can have great comfort knowing that He will do what He has promised.

Hebrews 6:18

If we are children of God, we will receive everything He has promised us. We will share with Christ all the things God has given to Him.

Romans 8:17

I pray that you will see how great the things are that He has promised to those who belong to Him.

Ephesians 1:18

"Know in all your hearts and in all your souls that not one of all the good promises the Lord your God made to you has been broken. All have come true for you. Not one of them has been broken."

JOSHUA 23:14

The eyes of the Lord are in every place, watching the bad and the good.

PROVERBS 15:3

"I am God and always will be. No one is able to take anything out of My hand. I do something, and who can change it?"

ISAIAH 43:13

He has promised us life that lasts forever!

1 JOHN 2:25

"You will keep the man in perfect peace whose mind is kept on You, because he trusts in You."

ISAIAH 26:3

We will receive the great things that we have been promised. They are being kept safe in heaven for us. They are pure and will not pass away. They will never be lost.

1 Peter 1:4

Even if I walk into trouble, You will keep my life safe. You will put out Your hand against the anger of those who hate me. And Your right hand will save me.

Psalm 138:7

"See, I am with you. I will care for you everywhere you go. . . . For I will not leave you until I have done all the things I promised you."

Genesis 28:15

"Know then that the Lord your God is God, the faithful God. He keeps His promise and shows His loving-kindness to those who love Him and keep His Laws, even to a thousand family groups in the future."

Deuteronomy 7:9

Dear God, I'm grateful for Your promises. Thank You for showing me that because You are my God, I never have to worry or be afraid of anything. You are in control of everything. I trust and believe that You love me and will never leave me. Even if I don't feel You near me, I know You are there, protecting me and doing what is right and best for me.

On bad days, and every day, I will come to You for wisdom and strength. Whatever kind of hard things I face, I know You will fix it. I will put my faith in You and believe that You make all things right at just the right time.

Thank You, God, for being there on the bad days and every day in between. I love You. Amen.